W. B. YEATS's SECOND PUBERTY

William Butler Yeats, 1932.
Prints and Photographs Division, Library of Congress

W. B. YEATS'S SECOND PUBERTY

A lecture delivered at the
Library of Congress
on April 2, 1984

by Richard Ellmann

Library of Congress   Washington   1985

Library of Congress Cataloging in Publication Data
Ellmann, Richard, 1918-
  W. B. Yeats's second puberty.

    Supt. of Docs. no.: LC 1.2:Y3
    1. Yeats, W. B. (William Butler), 1865-1939—Biography
—Last years and death—Addresses, essays, lectures.
2. Yeats, W. B. (William Butler), 1865-1939—Criticism
and interpretation—Addresses, essays, lectures.
3. Authors, Irish—20th century—Biography—Addresses,
essays, lectures.   I. Title.
PR5906.E397   1985   821'.8 [B]   84-25088
ISBN 0-8444-0486-1

*Unless otherwise specified, photographs are courtesy of the
Special Collections Department, Robert W. Woodruff Library,
Emory University.*

Available from the Library of Congress, Central Services Division,
Washington, D.C. 20540

The Gertrude Clarke Whittall
Poetry and Literature Fund

The Gertrude Clarke Whittall Poetry and Literature Fund was established in the Library of Congress in December 1950, through the generosity of Mrs. Gertrude Clarke Whittall, in order to create a center in this country for the development and encouragement of poetry, drama, and literature. Mrs. Whittall's earlier benefactions include the presentation to the Library of a number of important literary manuscripts, a gift of five magnificent Stradivari instruments, the endowment of an annual series of concerts of chamber music, and the formation of a collection of music manuscripts that has no parallel in the Western Hemisphere.

The Poetry and Literature Fund allows the Library to offer poetry readings, lectures, and dramatic performances. This lecture is published by the Library to reach a wider audience and as a contribution to literary history and criticism.

W. B. YEATS, and not I, described his last years as a second puberty. He meant the term to express his renewed sexual vigor, though he thought of it as also a psychological recovery. Just after his marriage, when he was fifty-two, he had written in a poem, "I have as healthy flesh and blood as any rhymer's had," yet things had changed by the time he reached sixty-eight. At that time, in 1934, he complained to a friend that his sexual powers had diminished. The friend, as much in jest as in earnest, remarked that an Austrian physiologist, Eugen Steinach, had developed in 1918 an operation for rejuvenation. It had become popular in the 1920s. In Vienna, for example, a hundred teachers and university professors had submitted to the operation, one of them being Freud in 1923. Yeats promptly went to the library to consult the one book in English that dealt with it, *Rejuvenation* (1924), by the London surgeon Norman Haire. Haire wrote that he himself at that time had performed twenty-five such operations, with what he regarded as generally good results. The operation lasted only a quarter of an hour. No monkey glands took part. It was what we now know as a vasectomy: the surgeon cut the vas deferens, removed a piece of it, then tied up the two ends separately. Steinach's theory, which I am sorry to say is no longer held, was that the production of the male hormone would thereby be increased and vitalize the whole body's functioning.

Norman Haire was a well-known figure in London sexological circles. Yeats went to consult him and told him—as Haire wrote to me twelve years later—"that for about three years . . . he had lost all inspiration and been unable to write anything new. He had gone over varying versions of his poems, choosing those he preferred." To rescue his verse as well as his potency, then, Yeats thought he must undergo the operation. (He spoke also of improving his blood pressure.) Versemaking and lovemaking had always made connections in his mind. Not to be able to do the one meant not to be able to do the other. In a late poem he declares that the spur of his poetry has always been lust and rage, the same qualities which in "Byzantium" he speaks of as "the fury and the mire of human veins." What awakened his images to life, he insisted in a song for *The King of the Great Clock Tower*, was "heroic wantonness."

Haire operated on his distinguished patient during the first week of April 1934. Was it a success? Yeats thought that it was and must have encouraged his friend, the poet Sturge Moore, to have it two years later. On the physical level it cannot have had much effect, for Norman Haire, whom Yeats authorized to discuss his case, said to me what a woman friend of Yeats's confirmed—my curiosity was I hope legitimized by my being one of Yeats's biographers—that the operation had no effect upon his sexual competence. He could not have erections, Haire told me. But the effect on his mind, as Mrs. Yeats emphasized to me eight years after his death, was incalculable. Subsequent to the operation Yeats wrote to Norman Haire that "he had written new poems which, in the opinion of those whose opinion he valued most, were among his best work." These were poems included in the volume called A *Full Moon in March.*

The operation alarmed Yeats's friends. Frank O'Connor imagined that it was like putting a Cadillac engine in a Ford car. Yeats supposed that it had put an additional strain on his constitution. In a letter to Dorothy Wellesley of June 17, 1935, a letter she omitted from their published correspondence, he wrote, "I find my present weakness made worse by the strange second puberty the operation has given me, the ferment that has come upon my imagination. If I write more poetry it will be unlike anything I have done." He was projecting the volume we know as *Last Poems*, in which he would speak as "a wild old wicked man," "a foolish passionate man," and express what he called "an old man's frenzy," a frenzy that privileged him to speak out.

Yeats had only five years to live. He craved sexual intimacy and found several women willing to share it, whatever its limitations, yet he was always the writer, doing things as much "for the song's sake" as for other reasons. His wife said to him, "When you are dead people will talk about your love affairs, but I shall say nothing, for I will remember how proud you were." He was determined to make his last years count. What I shall contend is that they constitute, notwithstanding all the reverberations of a long lifetime, a distinct period, a phase in which he treats old subjects with greater explicitness and freedom and greater awareness of ultimate implications. He seems determined to cultivate extravagance, as if at their utmost bound things took on at last their true shapes and colors.

In *Last Poems* Yeats presents a polymorphous spectrum of sexual possibility. For example, there are two pairs of ideal lovers, Peleus and Thetis and the Irish Baile and Ailinn, whose resurrected bodies recreate their old earthy passions. On this side of mortality, too, the same impulses seek or achieve satisfaction. Yeats's spokesman is often an old man who ranges from longing to be young again and to hold a girl in his arms to swishing around with a pretty punk, chatting with an old bawd, and claiming to be "a young man in the dark." When Yeats takes up his old beloved Maud Gonne, always the central figure in his poetical enterprise, he does something with her that he has never done before—he names her. For the first time, as she waits for a train at Howth station, she is taken out of legend for a moment and put into life. The same candor appears in his vocabulary. Cuchulain's wife is now given the Homeric epithet of "great-bladdered Emer." Long before Yeats had been bold enough to speak of "the worse devil that is between my thighs," but now, in "The Three Bushes," he talks even more explicitly of "the lover's rod and its butting head," and describes it after intercourse as "weak as a worm." In the Crazy Jane poems he had spoken grandly and latinately of "the place of excrement"; in the *Last Poems* this becomes just "bum":

> Foul goat-head, brutal arm appear,
> Belly, shoulder, bum,
> Flash fishlike; nymphs and satyrs
> Copulate in the foam.

Such diversions go on in heaven itself, Yeats reports in "News for the Delphic Oracle," as if heaven too had had a Steinach operation performed by the poet himself.

He salts other subjects in the same way. Long ago he had celebrated the Easter Rebellion of 1916, memorialized its martyrs, and proclaimed that because of it "A terrible beauty is born." Now, in the 1930s, he finds nothing to praise in the regime of the Easter rebel, De Valera, whom like Maud Gonne he names. His attitude towards fascism is similar. He imagined briefly that Ireland might have found a worthier leader in General O'Duffy, leader of the Blue Shirts, but soon turned against him and wrote, "What if there's nothing up there at the top?" For good measure, in a poem addressed to those clerics and fascists who supposed that strengthening church and state would put down the mob, he wrote,

> But what if Church and the State
> Are the mob that howls at the door!

Not content with this, Yeats wrote still another poem dissociating himself from all governments, "The Great Day":

> Hurrah for revolution and more cannon-shot!
> A beggar upon horseback lashes a beggar on foot.
> Hurrah for revolution and cannon come again!
> The beggars have changed places, but the lash goes on.

The elegiac tone with which in the twenties he had lamented the loss of the old order changes to a kind of lambasting of "the sort now growing up, / All out of shape from toe to top," including aristocracy, middle class, and peasants alike.

The five years left to Yeats following the Steinach operation were a period of great literary fecundity. He wrote a series of works in prose and verse. There were four verse plays, more outspoken than their predecessors. The first, A *Full Moon in March*, centered on the beheading of a poet. Then *The Herne's Egg* dealt with the rape of a priestess by seven men. In *Purgatory* an old man, who long ago killed his father, now kills his own son. In *The Death of Cuchulain*, the figure whose heroic deeds Yeats had celebrated in other plays dies at last with more indignity than glory at a fool's hand. Yeats now composed the last section of his *Autobiographies* and varied his usual loftiness of tone by a gossipy exposure of the foibles of George Moore. He also compiled *The Oxford Book of Modern Verse*, in which he praised and dispraised various contemporaries to excess and—in this most tendentious of all the Oxford Books—included great swatches of obscure poets to whom he alone was partial. He prepared, too, a collected edition of his writings and, in an introduction to it, surprised his potential readers by such remarks as, "I am no nationalist, except in Ireland for passing reasons"—this from a lifelong nationalist who in his last poems would speak of "We Irish" and address himself to "Irish poets" as if he were very much one of them. In what he intended to be the first installment of a series called *On the Boiler*—the title drawn from a recollection of a ship's carpenter who harangued from on top of a boiler in Sligo—Yeats polemicized against modern education, plumped for eugenics, and in general claimed to be discarding his usual "patter" in favor of the fanaticism which it had always overlain. No statement was too willful: he announced that a small Irish army "could throw back from our shores the disciplined unedu-

W. B. Yeats, about 1905

cated masses of the commercial nations." Mrs. Yeats told me that in the second number of *On the Boiler,* which he did not live to write, he intended to fulminate against all institutional religions.

This sounds like "a wild old man" indeed, and yet Yeats is so inevitably a writer that neither his art nor his audience seems ever in danger of being forgotten. One of his principal undertakings in his last years was to prepare a new edition of his book *A Vision,* the most eccentric of all his writings. The first edition, published in 1926, contained two sections that were in finished form, but much of the rest was tangled and inchoate. Yeats felt that he had to bring the book up to the standard and the spirit of his final period. That a book called *A Vision* should be subject to revision might seem absurd, though perhaps not more so than the idea mocked by Thomas Paine in *The Age of Reason,* of attributing two testaments to God. In revising it Yeats reconceived of the book as a whole.

A Vision had begun in 1917 when, during their honeymoon, Mrs. Yeats sought to divert her husband from disquieting thoughts about having married the wrong woman by attempting automatic writing. Originally a marital stratagem, the automatic writing suddenly took off in startling new directions. It offered, in fragments, a symbology far more complicated than any Yeats had come to on his own, and yet it roughly jibed with his previous thoughts. The manner of the revelation was somewhat embarrassing: it was one thing to be a mystic, and another to be a mystic's consort. Mrs. Yeats had no wish to be presented to the world as a Pythoness, and her husband could hardly claim to be his own oracle. Moreover, he felt that his readers would be put off by the idea of spooky communicators. So when he first brought out the book, instead of claiming authorship or joint authorship, he offered a little facade of mystery. The title page of the 1926 *Vision* read: A *Vision: An Explanation of Life Founded upon the Writings of Giraldus Cambrensis and upon Certain Theories Attributed to Kusta Ben Luka.* Needless to say, neither of these worthies had anything to do with the book. Yet it would have been hard for a reader to know for certain whether Yeats was fooling or not, or why he should wish to dissimulate.

For the second edition he resolved to tell the true story of how the book came into being. Mrs. Yeats said to me that this decision provoked the most painful quarrel, perhaps the only serious one, of their marriage. She wanted him to publish the book straight-forwardly, without explanation or preliminaries. But Yeats evidently felt that to do so would be to promulgate the Tables of the Law without the necessary preliminary of ascending Mount Sinai. Besides, the actual origin of the book was as fabulous as any concocted claim of Giraldus's or Kusta's help.

So in the 1937 edition Yeats owned up publicly to his domestic Delphi. The fact that the book had developed out of his marriage bed gave it that blend of love, beauty, and wisdom which he had always sought. He also reconceived its nature. It was not a new religion, it was not a philosophy; it was a symbological myth. "One can believe in a myth," Yeats said, "one can only assent to a philosophy." Believing in his own myth did not come quite so easy as that, however. Yeats pondered this question and as early as 1928 composed what he called "A Packet for Ezra Pound," which was a kind of dedication of the book to the man who would be least likely to accept it. The first *Vision* had been dedicated to a fellow-occultist, the second was packeted to a sceptic. The appropriateness of using Pound was that, if Yeats could make his book seem sensible to someone of a different school, he might speak with more authority. It had occurred to him that Pound's explanation of the structural scheme of the *Cantos*, which he had heard at Rapallo, bore at least some resemblance to his own structural scheme in *A Vision*. Coming from different ends of the intellectual scene, they had unwittingly found common ground. Yeats concluded the "Packet to Ezra Pound" with four extraordinary sentences:

Some will ask whether I believe in the actual existence of my circuits of sun and moon. Those that include, now all recorded time in one circuit, now what Blake called "the pulsation of an artery," are plainly symbolical, but what of those that fixed, like the butterfly upon a pin, to our central date, the first day of our Era, divide actual history into periods of equal length? To such a question I can but answer that if sometimes, overwhelmed by miracle as all men must be when in the midst of it, I have taken such periods literally, my reason has soon recovered; and now that the system stands out clearly in my imagination I regard them as stylistic arrangements of experience comparable to the cubes in the drawing of Wyndham Lewis and to the ovoids in the sculpture of Brancusi. They have helped me to hold in a single thought reality and justice.

Only reality and justice! When Yeats began the paragraph, he seemed about to make a modest disclaimer of literal truth and of preternatural assistance, but as he went along, he insisted that the *Vision* had come to him miraculously, and at the end, in a sentence rewritten in his final period, he claims more than literal truth, he claims to have gathered together reality and justice. What appeared to be a partial retraction turned into an even more extravagant claim.

Still, Yeats did not dash immediately from "A Packet for Ezra Pound" into the system itself. He must have felt that it would come all too suddenly upon readers not disposed to accept it, so he added a section, "Stories of Michael Robartes and His Friends," to predispose them in his favor. He had pretended that Giraldus and Kusta were actual sources, which they were not; the new stories of Robartes were not presented as anything but extravaganzas. One, which involved cuckoos and cuckolding, had been written in 1928. But the other, written in his last period, was closer to his feelings after the Steinach operation. It was based on something that had happened in Oxford in the early 1920s. As he informed Dorothy Wellesley on July 26, 1936, "We let our house in the Broad, Oxford, to some American girl students. In the middle of the night Alan Porter (later editor or sub-editor of *The Spectator*) climbed through the window. He was welcomed but found to be impotent. He explained that he had a great friend and when that friend had tired of a girl [he] had always taken her for himself. If he found a girl for himself he was impotent. The student said fetch your friend. He did. And after that all went well . . . I have worked it up into a charming fantasy of shyness. If the girl lay with the friend he felt she belonged to the family: once was enough."

Impotence was clearly a great subject for Yeats, even during his second puberty. In *A Vision* he has this story told by the young woman who calls herself Denise de l'Isle Adam, as something that has happened to her. The absurd name she bears is of course based upon that of Villiers de l'Isle Adam, the author of the symbolist drama *Axël*, which fascinated Yeats as a young man. In that play, Axël, on the grounds that life cannot possibly live up to their hopes for it, persuades the heroine to die with him at once rather than consummate their love and experience inevitable disappoint-

14

W. B. Yeats with his family in the 1920s

ment. In Yeats's idealistic youth, this antiphysical play had meant a good deal to him, and in his own play *The Shadowy Waters*, the lovers behave rather similarly. But Denise, in the course of recounting her own experience, comments that Axël in Villiers' play was motivated not by scorn of life and sexuality but by shyness and temporary impotence. This is a worldly wise revision of the solemnity of *Axël*, in keeping with Yeats's later manner and outlook. And yet the story is not merely one of corporeal accommodation. It implies something else, that Denise loves one man with her soul and accepts the other with her body. The soul may keep its distance while the body embraces, and vice versa. The same theme animates Yeats's late group of poems, "The Three Bushes," where the mistress is averse to physical but not to spiritual love and asks her serving maid to substitute covertly for her in the dark with her lover, while she loves him spiritually in the light. The maid, however, loves him body and soul. So this bawdy tale had its metaphysical side, as in fact all sexuality has for Yeats from beginning to end, with the body usually proving the soul's power.

15

When it came to the avowedly mystical materials of A *Vision*, Yeats left alone the sections of the first *Vision* that dealt with psychology and with cultural history, only omitting an indiscreet prophecy of the immediate future. He concentrated his revision upon the sections that dealt with the metaphysical aspect of the self and with the afterlife. These sections had originally been full of admissions of uncertainty, which Yeats now largely deleted. He set a more confident tone, and made much more frequent resort to metaphors. But in a way these sections could never be finished. The more he refined them, the more he came up against central problems that he could not solve without pretending to more certainty than he had. The principal ones were the relation of the human self to its spiritual counterpart, a sort of ethereal alter ego, and the battle between free will and determinism. For the first, Yeats had a theory about the spirits, which he expressed most fully in a note called "Seven Propositions," never published by him. The first proposition holds that "Reality is a timeless and spaceless community of Spirits which perceive each other. Each Spirit is determined by and determines those it perceives, and each Spirit is unique." The second states, "When these Spirits reflect themselves in time and space they still determine each other, and each Spirit sees the others as thoughts, images, objects of sense. Time and space are unreal."

The obvious difficulty with these two propositions, and with the five others that I shall not rehearse, is that, if the Spirits alone are real, human beings have only a provisional, precarious existence. In other words, Yeats was reversing our usual assumption that spirits are shadowy creatures, human beings substantial ones, and instead making men and women shadowy and the spirits substantial. Much of Yeats's verse had tried to body forth the spirit world and spiritualize the natural one. But it was always couched in such a way that it could be taken as extravagant metaphor, emotionally warranted rather than doctrinally justified. He could not quite concede to flesh and blood the minor role which his theory seemed to accord them. As a result, he not only limited the autonomy of the spirits in A *Vision*, but in the verse written at the same time he suggested that the spirits were jealous of the human and longed to be bodied so as to undergo "desecration and the lover's night." In his early verse the fairies kidnap human children out of the same jealousy of the mortal condition, and the gods—Celtic or Greek—fall in love with them and rape or seduce them.

The second problem in the book, free will as opposed to determinism, Yeats also left open. So though A *Vision* has the semblance of a deterministic system, in which past and future obey mechanical laws and beings occupy their allotted and fixed places on a wheel, Yeats—once he had perfected the system—gave play to what he called the Thirteenth Cone or Sphere, a kind of god-surrogate who can alter everything. By introducing the unpredictable into a system predicated on predictability, Yeats kept the relation of physical and metaphysical forever wavering. So these two great issues—of spirit and substance, of freedom and compulsion—were left as blurred in the second *Vision* as they had been in the first. Yeats refused to close the system. He did not mind that there were loose ends in it. The editor who dealt with the book for the Macmillan Company, Thomas Mark, once told me (and bound me to secrecy) that he had pointed out to Yeats some small inconsistencies in A *Vision*; to his surprise Yeats showed no special concern. It was as if he knew that the symbology would always be imperfect.

After the publication of the second *Vision*, Yeats began to express some dissatisfaction with it. In "A General Introduction to My Work," he said that "subconscious preoccupation" with the theme of Unity of Being "brought me A *Vision*, its harsh geometry an incomplete interpretation." By this time, it was not *Mrs.* Yeats's subconscious, but Yeats's—she had been demoted to being simply an agent of his subconscious mind. "I don't know whether I want my friends to see it," he wrote. In a letter to Ethel Mannin he called A *Vision* his "public philosophy," and said he had a "private philosophy" as well. At one time A *Vision* had been private, but now it was merely exoteric, and there were ideas far more intimate that he had not revealed. His private philosophy, he informed Ethel Mannin, was "the material dealing with individual mind which came to me with that on which the mainly historical *Vision* is based. I have not published it because I only half understand it."

I think we can surmise at least some of the topics which Yeats's private philosophy included. So we might shadow forth still another vision, a third one, the one he never wrote down. This one seems to underlie all his work, but only as he reached the end of his life did he fully acknowledge it. More than ever before he recognized certain problems as having more than one solution, and thought his best course must be to register rather than resolve his conflicting responses to them.

What could dissatisfy him about A Vision was not so much its incoherence upon ultimate matters but its sanguine air. The eternal round goes on, "birth is heaped on birth," the soul undergoes its appointed metamorphoses; all seems neat and ongoing. In one section Yeats rebukes Paul Valéry for having rejoiced, in Le Cimitière marin, that all life must pass. No, he says, he prefers to remember a young woman (Maud Gonne's daughter Iseult) who sang on a Normandy beach a song of her own composition in which each verse ended, "O Lord, let something remain." Yet Yeats was not always so life-affirming. In his own poem "Vacillation," he imagined a Chinese warlord saying to battleweary men, "Let all things pass away." Desire is balanced by scornful renunciation. If A Vision had no place for such sentiments, that was one of its shortcomings.

Yeats explicitly acknowledged that one subject he had neglected in A Vision was what he called "the beatific vision." In a way this was the cornerstone of the whole system, because the point of almost endless becoming is to achieve at last true unified being. Had Yeats written in his prose book what he expressed in his verse, he would have discoursed on the several forms that beatitude may take: there is the unity of lovers, achieved by a communion of minds and bodies; there is the unity achieved by a communion of minds and bodies; there is the positive unity achieved by heroes at the culmination of their exploits, and the negative unity achieved by saints at the culmination of their sufferings; there is the unity which souls may achieve after death; there is the unity achieved by works of art out of gross matter; and there is another unity, a more unassuming one, which sometimes steals upon us unawares in casual circumstances, not less momentous for being unsought. Each of these states defied and transcended the usual condition of life. That condition Yeats always framed as a conflict of contraries.

But the beatific vision could be only one end of the seesaw. The other was its obverse, a vision which nullified all that the beatific vision offered. Instead of completeness, there was blankness. Instead of enterprise, there was futility. In his youth Yeats had envis-

W. B. Yeats with his wife in Rapallo after suffering from Malta fever, about 1928

aged the coming of the rose as a benign renaissance, but he had also envisaged the coming of malign destruction in "The Valley of the Black Pig." In his later work, though he never forsook the idea of renaissance completely, his prophecies had often an element of terror. The avatar of "The Second Coming" is a dreadful medley of man and beast, and slouches towards Bethlehem as a symbol of the Antichrist who will destroy all that has been begotten. Threats of God burning time, or of the poet setting a match to the time world because it failed to measure up to his standard for it, had always provided a negative undertone in Yeats's generally affirming verse. His conception of the afterlife offered a comparable doubleness. In "The Cold Heaven," souls are punished with injustice instead of justice, heaven becomes hell. This poem was the opposite of a late poem such as "John Kinsella's Lament for Mistress Mary Moore," where we are told of heaven, "No expectation fails there, / No pleasing habit ends." The afterlife might or might not be benign.

When Yeats considered love from the obverse point of view it no longer stood as a symbol of completeness but as a locked relationship of torturer and victim, of love and hate. So "Her Vision in the Wood" is much closer to Baudelaire than to Dante, and in a late poem he speaks of hatred of God as a sentiment just as inspiring as love of God. His attitude towards art had also two aspects. Long ago, in 1925, he had written in "Sailing to Byzantium" of the longing of an old man to break out of detested nature and into the perfection of art. His friend Sturge Moore reminded him that art is itself natural, and Yeats agreed by writing his second poem, "Byzantium," in which also the emphasis comes upon the wonderful transformation which art effects upon life's images. But in his final period Yeats took up the subject again, in "The Circus Animals' Desertion." This time he put Byzantium aside, as if to deal with the problem more directly. He began by convoking his own earlier artistic images and pointed out that they had their origin in sexual passion but took on gradually an independent life. It might seem that this poem, like those about Byzantium, would celebrate the purifying and distancing power of art. But in the last stanza Yeats suddenly turns around and declares:

> Those masterful images because complete
> Grew in pure mind, but out of what began?
> A mound of refuse or the sweepings of a street,
> Old kettles, old bottles, and a broken can,
> Old iron, old bones, old rags, that raving slut
> Who keeps the till. Now that my ladder's gone,
> I must lie down where all the ladders start,
> In the foul rag-and-bone shop of the heart.

Vaunt its mastery as it will, art must depend from the welter of unpurified experience, and that crude welter, like "the frog-spawn of a blind man's ditch"—his image for life in "A Dialogue of Self and Soul"—grips us again with its detestable fascination.

"The Circus Animals' Desertion" deals with the genesis of art but does not question its authority. It remains for another late poem of Yeats, "What Then?," to do that. In "What Then?" the old man surveys a life of high literary achievement:

> "The work is done," grown old he thought,
> "According to my boyish plan;
> Let the fools rage, I swerved in naught,
> Something to perfection brought";

Plato's ghost, who has raised his quizzical cry, "What Then?," after each stanza, sings it even louder this time. "But louder sang that ghost, 'What then?'" The seeming victories of art over time may be as meaningless as any other illusion.

What Yeats questions in art he also questions in life. Usually he praised life, though often grudgingly or defiantly. But there were moments when he could see, obversely, an ultimate emptiness. His late poem "Meru" is one of the most telling expressions of this idea:

> Civilization is hooped together, brought
> Under a rule, under the semblance of peace
> By manifold illusion; but man's life is thought,
> And he, despite his terror, cannot cease
> Ravening through century after century,
> Ravening, raging, and uprooting that he may come
> Into the desolation of reality.

Beatifically, reality is where "all the barrel hoops are knit," according to Yeats's poem "There," but obversely, as in "Meru," the hoops will not hold, and what we have is "desolation." "Egypt and Greece, good-bye, and good-bye, Rome!" is the splendid dismissal of the pretensions of civilizations to escape from nothingness. In "Meru" Yeats attributes this recognition to the East, and in another late poem, "The Statues," declares, "Grimalkin crawls to Buddha's emptiness" (that is, a worshipper who is nothing crawls to a god who is nothing, too). The East is a hemisphere of his own mind as well as a geographical entity. In "The Black Tower," Yeats evokes the tower which he had used often before with all kinds of iconic meanings, but this time the terrible possibility of its meaninglessness appears even to its defenders. "The Pilgrim" in a poem of that name has fasted, made the pilgrimage to Lough Derg, questioned the dead, and now summarizes all that he has learned as "fol de rol de rolly O"—meaninglessness with a lilt.

This obverse vision makes itself felt in Yeats's last poems perhaps most notably in regard to death. As befitted a man grown old, the poems are full of the dead, the dying, the about to die. His son recalls that the doctors had given Yeats only three years to live, and that he had told his wife, "I am disgracing the family by dying so young." The subject was one he had often contemplated earlier. Twenty years before, in a group of poems about Aubrey Beardsley's sister Mabel, Yeats had praised those who laugh "into the face of death." In "Lapis Lazuli," which comes in his final volume, he describes the death of various tragic heroes, especially Hamlet and Lear, and attributes to them not exactly laughter but a sort of tragic gaiety. (He does the same in his prose work *On the Boiler*.) The actors who play Hamlet and Lear are right in not weeping at the

21

W. B. Yeats telling a joke, sometime in the 1930s

moment of their stage deaths, because Hamlet and Lear have expressed fundamental energies and these, as Blake said and Yeats quoted, are "eternal delight." Another way of putting this would be that they complete their images of themselves at the very moment that death strikes: "Blackout: Heaven blazing into the head." Yeats liked to talk of a Norse god who died as a sacrifice to himself. Tragic heroes, in pursuing their destiny to its end, make death their accomplice rather than their adversary.

Against this view of death as a means of tragic illumination, joyfully received, which many poems uphold, there is an obverse view that it may be nothing of the sort. Occasionally Yeats expresses this. If in "Under Ben Bulben" Yeats could assure his readers that death is only a momentary interruption before the soul is again reincarnated, he offers no such consolation in another poem, "The Apparitions." Here the refrain, based as Mrs. Yeats told me upon an actual nightmare of Yeats which he interpreted to be about death, only repeats,

> Fifteen apparitions have I seen;
> The worst a coat upon a coat-hanger.

Perhaps the gloomiest of all Yeats's poems is the very late one "The Man and the Echo." Like a number of his other poems, it is a debate, but this time the adversary is not self nor soul nor heart nor antiself, but a hollow and defeatist echo. It begins with the man remorsefully reviewing things he has misdone or failed to do:

> And all seems evil until I
> Sleepless would lie down and die.

To which Echo responds without pity,

> Lie down and die.

But the man refuses to accept this solution. He is full of humanistic affirmation:

> That were to shirk
> The spiritual intellect's great work . . .
> While man can still his body keep
> Wine or love drugs him to sleep . . .
> But body gone he sleeps no more,
> And till his intellect grows sure
> That all's arranged in one clear view,
> Pursues the thoughts that I pursue,
> Then stands in judgment on his soul,
> And, all work done, dismisses all
> Out of intellect and sight
> And sinks at last into the night.

W. B. Yeats with Edith Shackleton Heald, who was a late mistress, and Mrs. Edmund Dulac (seated right), about 1938. Yeats's poem on nothing was dictated to Edith Shackleton Heald and then signed by him.

To which Echo answers only,
> Into the night.

In desperation at this blankness, the man cries,
> O Rocky Voice,
> Shall we in that great night rejoice?

In these lines Yeats recalls the first poem in his final volume, "The Gyres," in which he had declared,

> Out of cavern comes a voice
> And all it knows is that one word, "Rejoice!"

But in "The Man and the Echo," the man answers his almost hopeless question with an even more hopeless one, still addressed to Echo:
> What do we know but that we face
> One another in this place?

This time Echo does not have to answer. To the obverse vision, any idea that life and afterlife make sense cannot be sustained. So Yeats, who had claimed at the end of his book A *Vision* to hold in a single thought reality and justice, was obliged by his inner honesty to allow for the possibility that reality was desolation and justice a figment.

Mrs. Yeats told me that it would have taken her husband a hundred years to complete his work. I surmise that he was roughening the edges of the two forces he had always seen at work in the world, the one looking at reality askance as something temporary, provisional, and tidal, the other regarding it as hive or nest-like, tenacious, lasting. In May 1938 he dictated but never published a quatrain which was sold at Christies in 1978. In this poem the first line questioned, "What is the explanation of it all?" and the following lines went on,

> What does it look like to a learned man?
> Nothings in nothings whirled, or when he will,
> From nowhere into nowhere nothings run.

Perhaps in no other poem did Yeats take the obverse of the beatific vision so darkly. But the word nothing resounds in two of his late plays: the old man in *Purgatory* says at the end, "Twice a murderer and all for nothing," and the last speech of *The Herne's Egg* memorializes blankness, "All that trouble and nothing to show for it . . . ." Long before Yeats had written, "Where there is nothing, there is God," but he had also had King Fergus say, "Now I have grown

W. B. *Yeats in the 1930s*

nothing, knowing all." In another late work, "The Gyres," Yeats indicated that "out of any rich dark nothing" the whole gazebo could be built up once again. He could conceive of nothing as empty and also as pregnant. I think he saw with increasing sharpness the clash between the urge to have done with fine distinctions, subtle passions, and differentiated matter, and the urge to keep them at all costs. In his last play, *The Death of Cuchulain*, the final chorus asks,

> Are those things that men adore and loathe
>   Their sole reality?

As Yeats reached his life's end, he recognized that he would never be able to decide between the beatific vision and its obverse. The image of life as an abounding horn was relentlessly undermined by the image of life as an empty shell. In his last plays he allows the central characters to share in this sense of the indeterminable. The old man in *Purgatory* thinks that he can release his mother's soul from purgatory by killing his son only to discover that his ghastly deed has no effect. This play has been read as an elegy upon the decline of the Irish country house, but I think it should be read primarily as a lament for the impossibility of imposing the beatific vision upon its horrid obverse. The Steinach operation symbolized for Yeats his attempt to impose potency upon impotence, yet even as he claimed to be young he knew he was not. Pain and nullification accompanied him during the years that he lived out his second puberty. At the end we must, as he once said, "sing amid our uncertainty." In his youth he predicted in "The Man Who Dreamed of Faeryland" that one day God would "burn nature with a kiss." In a late letter he returned to this idea: "The last kiss is given to the void." The artist imposes form upon the void but knows that the void may yet overwhelm. In the fiery furnaces where universes are made they may also go to die. "The painter's brush consumes his dreams," Yeats wrote, and knew that the poet's pen belongs similarly to a process of decreation as much as of creation. A last letter of Yeats took comfort in one thing alone, that man if he cannot know the truth can at least embody it. Not without unconscious pride, he said he would embody it in the completion of his life. What he meant was that the great questions could be given only momentary answers, couched in passionate utterance. Visionaries or not, we are only, as Falstaff says, "mortal men, mortal men."

NOTE: I am grateful to Warwick Gould for giving me the text of Yeats's little poem about nothing, the original of which is now in his possession. Michael Yeats remembered some of his father's late utterances. Mrs. Yeats, Norman Haire, and Frank O'Connor also contributed their recollections from the past. John Kelly helped with Yeats's unpublished letters.

Other Publications on Literature Available from the Library of Congress

The following publications, based on lectures presented at the Library of Congress, are available free from the Library of Congress, Central Services Division, Washington, D.C. 20540. When ordering, please specify the title, author, and date of publication.

CARL SANDBURG by Mark Van Doren. With a bibliography of Sandburg materials in the collections of the Library of Congress. 1969. 83 p.

CHAOS AND CONTROL IN POETRY, a lecture by Stephen Spender. 1966. 14 p.

THE INSTANT OF KNOWING by Josephine Jacobsen. 1974. 14p.

JAMES JOYCE'S HUNDREDTH BIRTHDAY: SIDE AND FRONT VIEWS by Richard Ellmann. 1982. 33 p.

LITERARY LECTURES PRESENTED AT THE LIBRARY OF CONGRESS. 1973. 602 p.

LOUISE BOGAN: A WOMAN'S WORDS by William Jay Smith. With a bibliography. 1971. 81 p.

METAPHOR AS PURE ADVENTURE by James Dickey. 1968. 20 p.

OSCAR WILDE AT OXFORD by Richard Ellmann. 1984. 32 p.

THE PATHETIC FALLACY by Anthony Hecht. 1984. 28 p.

PORTRAIT OF A POET: HANS CHRISTIAN ANDERSEN AND HIS FAIRYTALES by Erik Haugaard. 1973. 17 p.

RANDALL JARRELL by Karl Shapiro. With a bibliography of Jarrell materials in the collections of the Library of Congress. 1967. 47 p.

THE REASONS FOR POETRY AND THE REASON FOR CRITICISM by William Meredith. 1982. 36 p.

ROBERT FROST: LECTURES ON THE CENTENNIAL OF HIS BIRTH. 1975. 74 p. "In- and Outdoor Schooling: Robert Frost and the Classics" by Helen Bacon, "Toward the Source: The Self-Realization of Robert Frost, 1911-1912" by Peter Davison, "Robert Frost's 'Enigmatical Reserve': The Poet as Teacher and Preacher" by Robert Pack, "Inner Weather: Robert Frost as a Metaphysical Poet" by Allen Tate.

ROBERT LOWELL by Anthony Hecht. 1984. 32 p.

SAINT-JOHN PERSE: PRAISE AND PRESENCE by Pierre Emmanuel. With a bibliography. 1971. 82 p.

THE TRANSLATION OF POETRY. Address by Allen Tate and panel discussion presented at the International Poetry Festival held at the Library of Congress, April 13-15, 1970. 1972. 40 p.

TWO LECTURES. 1973. 31 p. "Leftovers: a CARE Package" by William Stafford and "From Anne to Marianne: Some Women in American Poetry" by Josephine Jacobsen.

WALLACE STEVENS: THE POETRY OF EARTH by A. Walton Litz. 1981. 15 p.

WALT WHITMAN: MAN, POET, PHILOSOPHER. 1955, reissued 1969. 53 p. "The Man" by Gay Wilson Allen, "The Poet" by Mark Van Doren, "The Philosopher" by David Daiches

DESIGNED BY JOHN MICHAEL ROCKVILLE MARYLAND